THE WATERLOO - SOUTHAMPTON LINE

R.W. KIDNER

THE OAKWOOD PRESS
1983

INTRODUCTION

The Southampton line was the London & South Western Railway's first and perhaps most important line. Because of its many junctions, some with other railways, and the multifarious activities of the Port, it carried a wider mix of trains than most. It also offered in its middle section an excellent racing ground for engines. For these reasons it is felt that it deserves a study of its own, notwithstanding the many excellent histories of the L&SWR which have been published.

There were of course many ways of getting from Waterloo to Southampton without going all the way down the main line; these included the route via Aldershot, Alton and Winchester Junction, and nine of them were recognised by head-codes in the working books. However this survey is mainly confined to the straight route, with side-glances at the junctions whereby other routes were possible.

ISBN 085361 291 9

EARLY HISTORY: 1834–1849

The port of Southampton, though going back in history to before the Romans, was still small at the beginning of the nineteenth century. However, with its wealth of land-protected approaches and four tides in twenty-four hours, it had a natural attraction for sailing vessels from the west, for whom the long beat up the Channel to the Thames was slow and dangerous. First thoughts of connecting the port with the Capital were for a canal, but enthusiasm for this form of transport was waning; in 1830 a Southampton and London Rail Road Company prospectus was issued, and in 1831 another railway was proposed, the Southampton, London, and Branch Railway and Docks Co. This was followed in 1834 by a Bill for the London & Southampton Railway, which was approved by the Act of the same year (5 Will. IV c. 88). Although plans to bring railways right into (and indeed across) the City were being mooted, the L&S decided to opt for a terminus at Nine Elms, on the south bank of the Thames near Battersea, from which communication by boat to all parts of London would be easy. The first section of the new railway, to Woking Common, was opened to traffic on 21 May 1838.

Although the L&S obtained its Act only one year after the London & Birmingham, the latter has had more attention, and it is not always realised that the L&S was conceived and opened at a time when railways were unproved and almost experimental. For instance, the first time-table was laid out like a stage-coach poster, showing trains leaving Nine Elms at 8, 10, 1, half-past 3 and 6; and from Woking Common at 7, half-past 10, 1, 3 and 7. However, it also showed times for the intermediate stations at Wandsworth, Wimbledon, Kingston, Ditton Marsh, Walton and Weybridge. The first Engineer, Francis Giles, was replaced before the opening, in 1837, by Joseph Locke. True, the course had been laid out without many major engineering works, but this probably owed more to the terrain than the Engineer; in particular, there was some dispute over the method of passing through the high ground near Micheldever.

Working methods at Nine Elms seem to have been somewhat primitive; there was a respectable gradient up from the waterside to Longhedge Farm, and an employee of the time, talking 50 years later, stated that when trains had difficulty starting up this, horses were attached to help it. There would have been plenty of horses; early depots were arranged not so much around pointwork as around small turntables. Engines had to have their tenders uncoupled for turning, and carriages were moved sideways to make up trains. Muscle power of horses and men took a greater part in readying a train than steam did.

In 1839 the L&S had plans for a branch from Eastleigh to Gosport, and since the citizens of Portsmouth had no liking for a railway bearing the name of a rival port, the name was changed to London & South Western Railway. Meanwhile on 24 September 1838 operation had been extended to Shapley

(Winchfield), and on 10 June 1839 from there to Basingstoke, and also from Southampton to Winchester. The intervening portion, held up due to possible deviations, followed on 11 May 1840.

Just west of the later Earlsfield station the line crossed over the 1803 Surrey Iron Railway, which ran from Wandsworth to Croydon; this was, however, moribund and closed in 1846, being purchased by the L&SWR and then resold to the London & Brighton Railway, under an agreement whereby the latter might have got running powers from Earlsfield to Nine Elms, though this did not in fact happen. Near Farnborough the Basingstoke Canal passed over the line; this canal, which by use of the Wey Navigation allowed barges to pass from Basingstoke into the Thames, was the nearest thing the L&SWR had to competition at that time, apart from the stage-coaches and broad-wheeled carriers' carts.

June 10 1839 was chosen as 'opening day' although the line was not open throughout. Special trains ran from Waterloo to Basingstoke and from Southampton to Winchester. In the latter case the engine was *'Pegasus'*, and the trains comprised four carriages, the mail coach which had been working from the Royal Hotel to London placed on a flat truck, and some wagons with workmen. The initial service comprised six trains to Basingstoke and four to Woking. The stage-coach covering the 'gap' took 2 hours, and Southampton could be reached in 5 hours from London. The official tables quoted 'Vauxhall' as the starting point, not Nine Elms. There is an interesting record of an early trip in Francis Wishaw's 'Railways of Great Britain and Ireland' of 1840. On August 23 1839 he travelled from Winchester to Southampton in a train of two first class, two second, and two excursion

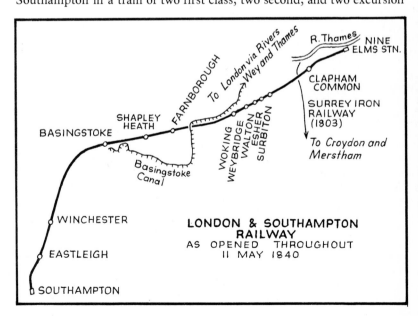

LONDON & SOUTHAMPTON RAILWAY
AS OPENED THROUGHOUT
11 MAY 1840

Waterloo station as it was when opened in 1848 (from the 'Illustrated London News' of 1 July 1848).

An early print of Basingstoke station, probably from Meason's Guide, 1856.

carriages, and a stage-coach and an omnibus on flat wagons. A speed of 31.57 mph was obtained on the 1 in 250 down from Winchester. On the return, the same rake of carriages was followed by an omnibus, a horse-box and a goods wagon, and 31.25 mph was attained on the level approaching the Winchester bank. The engine in both cases was *Locke*. Another interesting item from contemporary writing appears in Arthur Freeling's 'London & Southampton Railway Companion' (1839); it appears that south of Winchester the railway was cut through plague-pits, some dating from as early as 941 AD, and a few of these pits could still be seen in the sides of the cuttings.

Operation of the railway did not always go smoothly: there were two serious accidents, at Nine Elms on 17 October 1840, and at Kingston (Surbiton) on 16 October 1841; but such things were not uncommon when all depended upon the human factor and men worked long hours; both resulted from a failure to present a red light at the proper time. For locomotive power the company relied upon 2-2-2 tender engines from various makers. The carriages were of good quality for the time — though one contemporary writer referred to them as 'rattle and squeak' — and the 'thirds' were somewhat less Spartan than those on other lines in the south.

The grand simplicity of the line from Nine Elms to Southampton did not last long. By 7 February 1842 the branch from Bishopstoke (Eastleigh) to Gosport was open; on 29 July 1847 working began from Southampton to Blechynden, and on to Brockenhurst. Woking to Guildford was opened on 5 May 1845. At the London end traffic began feeding into the main line; from Richmond (joining at Battersea) on 27 July 1846, from Chertsey to Weybridge 14 February 1848, from Hampton Court to near Surbiton 1 February 1849. As early as 1854, the grisly freight was running from the Necropolis station at Waterloo to Brookwood Cemetery. Thereafter openings came thick and fast.

Only 8 years after full opening, the important step was taken of building the 'Metropolitan Extension'. This short line left the existing one just south of Nine Elms and ran mostly on embankment and brick arches to a new terminus in York Road near the end of Waterloo Bridge. By thus securing a terminus almost opposite the seats of political power, and naming it after a victory still fresh in the mind, the L&SWR gained status. It was opened on 11 July 1848.

By 1849 there were seventeen trains in the day leaving Waterloo on the main line. Five of these ran to Hampton Court, four to Guildford via Woking, and eight to Southampton. Of these last the slowest was the morning 'Govt' or Parliamentary train (the only one carrying third-class passengers) which took $3\frac{3}{4}$ hours. The two 'mails' took 2 hours 55 mins. and 2 hours 17 mins., the ordinary first- and second-class (three) about 3 hours, and the two 'expresses' 2 hours and 2 hours 10 mins. The fastest of these two stopped only at Farnborough, Basingstoke, Winchester and Bishopstoke Junction (Eastleigh). The Up service was similar, but the fastest express did it in 1 hour 50 mins. The actual nomenclature of the stations then open was as follows: Vauxhall, Clapham Common, Wimbledon, Malden, Kingston (later Surbiton), Esher & Claremont, Walton & Hersham, Weybridge Junction, Woking, Farnborough, Fleetpond (later Fleet), Winchfield, Basingstoke, Andover Road (later Micheldever), Winchester, Bishopstoke Junction (later Eastleigh). The mileages shown at the time differ in various places by as much as a mile from those adopted later; Bradshaw showed Southampton as 80 miles, not 79.

When the Waterloo station was opened, trains were controlled by a signal (then still rare). This comprised a red circle, within which was a rotatable black disc with a D-shaped hole cut out. When the whole thing was edge-on to the driver, both lines were clear; when it was face-on and the D at the bottom, both lines were blocked; if the D was at left or right, the respective line was clear and the other blocked.

DEVELOPMENT: 1850–1913

It is now necessary to look at what the Great Western Railway was doing. The L&SWR must have been less concerned with competitive threats than lines north of London, for there were no prize industrial areas to be fought over. The South Western was a line for farmers, military men, bishops and high class tourists. However, the four counties to the west were open for grabs, and the GWR was not likely to ignore them. Some skirmishing began in the early 'forties, and as a result, the L&SWR signed an agreement with the GWR that it would not promote any lines west of Salisbury or Dorchester, provided the other company did not pursue plans to reach Southampton. However, the waters were still fairly muddy; even the Midland Railway had promoted a 'Manchester & Southampton Railway,' parts of which later became the Midland & South Western Junction Railway, and what later became the Didcot, Newbury & Southampton Railway was also being urged; however this was killed off by the House of Commons in 1846, partly no doubt because a break of gauge would have been required at the intended junction at Micheldever. Relations between the L&SWR and GWR were remarkably cordial in the circumstances, and it was to be 25 years before the matter of Great Western entry into Southampton came up again.

At the London end, an event of some importance was the opening in 1863 of Clapham Junction, the importance lying not in the station itself but in the connections surrounding it. A railway with the cumbrous title of the Birmingham, Bristol and Thames Junction Railway, authorised in 1836, had planned a line from what is now Willesden to Battersea, but only got as far as Kensington (Addison Road). By 1845 the line was virtually derelict, but in 1859 the southwards extension was revived, as the West London Extension Railway. This quickly came to fruition, and with it Clapham Junction station, lying east of the L&SWR Clapham Common station, which was closed, and roughly on the site of the junction with the Richmond branch at

Falcon Lane. By this time the L&SWR was not alone here, for from 1858 an LBSC line from Battersea Wharf ran alongside to the south across Longhedge Farm and through an adjacent bridge under St. Johns Hill Road before swinging south. The WLER was jointly owned by the L&SWR, LBSCR, LNWR and GWR, and the junctions put in included (in addition to existing ones at Willesden with the LNWR and Wormwood Scrubs with the GWR), a spur facing Up at West London Junction, east of Clapham Junction station, one running into the Richmond Line platforms at the station, another passing under the complex to join the LBSC, and yet another connecting the Richmond Line spur with a branch from the LC&DR via Longhedge Junction. The only connection missing was one to the Southampton Line platforms at Clapham Junction, for which reason trains off the WLER to the Southampton line normally ran via the Richmond line platforms, East Putney and Wimbledon. This enabled trains to run without reversal to Southampton and Bournemouth from the GWR, LNWR, London, Chatham & Dover (later SE&CR), from the Great Northern Railway via Ludgate Hill, and from the LBSC via Longhedge Junction.

The only serious attempt to promote a rival GWR-dominated route to Southampton, the Didcot, Newbury & Southampton Railway, came in 1873. This was originally intended to join the L&SWR near Micheldever, but after much wrangling a junction at Shawford was substituted. Meanwhile interests in Southampton pursued a plan for an independent line all the way, and the DN&S actually purchased a large amount of land near Southampton West station, stretching half a mile up Hill Lane, and half-completed a viaduct over the main road. In 1883 the appointment of the famous Staats Forbes of the LC&DR to the DN&S Board seems to have brought some reality to bear, and all construction in Southampton was stopped. By this time the constructed part of the DN&S was approaching Winchester (Chesil) station (opened 1 May 1885), and after even more wrangling the remaining 2 miles to Shawford Junction was completed and opened on 1 October 1891. Through trains began, but engines were changed at Winchester until 1910, when some GW engines began to run through to Southampton. Most of the stretch from Shawford Junction to Winchester (Chesil) was still maintained and theoretically worked by the L&SWR, and its successor the Southern Railway therefore took over the maintenance of a line over which only GWR trains ran.

In January 1891 the L&SWR opened a station at the Royal Pier, Southampton. A line to the pier from near Terminus station already existed but was not suited to passenger trains. The station was built on a curve towards the end of the pier, adjacent to the booking office for the steamers then running to Ryde, Portsmouth and Cowes. Trains were short and worked by condensing engines as related later. Initial service was four trains and none on Sundays, but this was increased to six and in some years there were Sunday trains. The station closed in September 1914 due to the War. It is assumed that trains were shunted out of the Terminus and attached to the Docks engine near the Canute Road signal cabin. In the following year the

L. and S. W. R. Southampton Express.

A Bournemouth express about 1900, with an Adams 4-4-0 piloting a Drummond T9 class (E. Pouteau).

The old part of Waterloo station before the rebuilding. The crossovers in the foreground led onto the single line across the concourse to the SE&CR (Tuck's 'London Railway Stations' series, No. 9279).

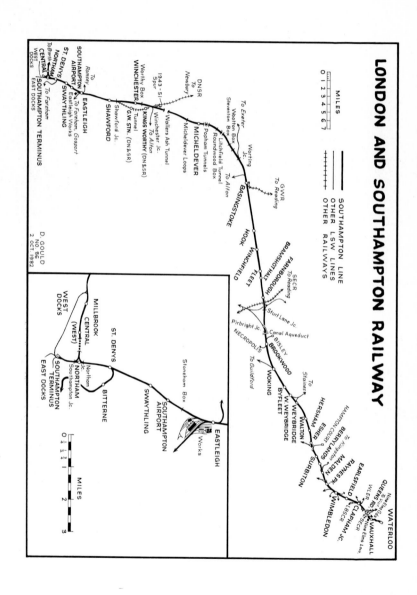

LONDON AND SOUTHAMPTON RAILWAY

D. GOULD
NO. 86
2 OCT. 1982

A ballast train passing Shawford Junction signal box about 1900.

The Royal Pier station at Southampton from the south.

3   SOUTHAMPTON — *View on Pier.* — LL.

L&SWR purchased Southampton Docks, clearing the way and providing the capital for the massive and continuous development of port installations and traffic which were to be a feature of the next forty years.

The London & South Western was more successful than some other lines in keeping its tracks sufficient for the traffic. This of course involved progressive widenings as well as other engineering works. The stretch from Basingstoke onwards was doubled by 1870; four tracks reached Basingstoke in 1905, and were extended to Worting in 1908. The fly-over at Battledown Junction (Worting) came into use in 1897, and in 1908 was re-arranged so that Southampton trains were diverted from the Down Fast to the Down Slow, which became the Southampton line, while Up trains from Southampton flew over the Salisbury line and a prolongation of the Up Southampton became the Up Slow, expresses going on to the centre Up Fast. These junctions were all laid out to take speeds up to 55 mph.

At the London end widenings and extensions of the Waterloo terminus took place at intervals. There was a major widening from Waterloo to Clapham Junction in 1877–84, and the junction at Malden was improved with the present fly-over system. Previously the Kingston line had burrowed under the main line west of Malden and then run to Wimbledon as a separate track on the south side.

By 1888 the direct line to Bournemouth from Brockenhurst via Sway was open, and the Holes Bay curve of 1893 enabled Weymouth trains to run direct without reversal. More of the trains were now taking the curve at Northam to Southampton West and beyond.

A development which had a marked effect on train timing and punctuality was the installation of electro-pneumatic signalling between Brookwood and Worting Junction. Sam Fay had brought the idea back from a visit to America, and put in a trial installation at Grateley in 1902. Soon afterwards work began on the Fleet section. A pump house was built there, with a steam engine supplying compressed air to a pipe running the whole length of the system. The signals, set up four at a time on gantries above the track, were worked by air pressure actuated electrically. Some intermediate gantries were arranged to change aspect automatically as the train passed, track circuiting being applied, probably for the first time in the UK. This system saved precious seconds as the expresses passed from section to section, and gave excellent service (apart from one tragic event described later), until replaced by colour-light signalling in 1966; the steam engine had been replaced by an electric pump in 1958.

In 1909 a complete reconstruction of the Waterloo terminus was begun, though it was not completed until 1922. Prior to 1909 the station had six lines leading into it, from south to north: Down Main, Up Local, Up Main, Down Windsor Slow, Down Windsor Fast, and Up Windsor. There were ten platforms (fifteen faces), and a centre track between the end of numbers 2 and 3 ran through the concourse to join the SE&CR. There was an engine shed on the south side with turntable, and a further turntable on the north side together with some carriage sidings. The Necropolis station lay on the

The famous 'A' signal box at Waterloo about 1908.

The view from the 'A' box in 1922 (Kingsway series, No. S14627).

south side just west of the 'A' signal box. As reconstructed, there were eight approach lines, from south to north: Down Local, Down Main, Up Relief, Up Main, Up Local, Down Windsor Slow, Down Windsor Fast, and Up Windsor. Platforms were increased to 21, the locomotive shed being abolished and the north turntable moved westwards. The 'A' box bridge was widened, and the Necropolis station moved westwards. The station buildings were almost entirely rebuilt, with the present wide steps and War Memorial being a central feature.

There have been conflicting statements in various sources about the number of platforms at Waterloo at various dates. Partly this may be due to the fact that until the 1909 rebuilding, all double-sided platforms carried only one number for both faces. By the time it was rebuilt it was certainly a hotch-potch. Platforms 1 to 3 (present 8 to 11) were the original station, with the ends of 2 and 3 modified in 1864 to feed into the single line across the concourse to the SER station. Platforms 4 to 6 (present 12 to 15) were added at the north-west side in 1860. In 1878 a South station was built south of the engine shed, but on the 1900 official plan this platform has no number. In 1885 yet more platforms were added at the north-west corner, platforms 7 to 10 (present 16 to 21). However contemporary photos show a notice 'to the Windsor and North Platforms 3, 4, 5, 6, 7, 8, 9,' and a photograph of the same date shows what would have been platform 10 used for milk traffic. Acworth in 'The Railways of England' 1889 states that there were 19 platforms which is hard to reconcile. The present platforms 1 to 7 were built over the site of the engine shed and South station during the rebuilding.

A feature of the station was the 'A' signal box straddling all lines at the Down end of the longest platforms. This was set up in 1892 (replacing an earlier one), with six gantries each carrying three 'branches'. Originally there were 41 signal arms, but later photographs of the box show these reduced to 26. The box was much modified over the years, and replaced in October 1936 by an all-electric box at the north-west corner of the station. The other well-known signal box at Waterloo, the 'Crows' Nest' over platforms 2 and 3, opened in 1874, was swept away in 1911 during the rebuilding.

THE PEAK YEARS: 1914–1948

The outbreak of War in 1914 found the L&SWR embarked on a programme of electrification of suburban services; some were completed in 1915-16, but no further progress was made until 1925. The Company was immediately heavily embroiled in War preparations, especially at Southampton from which the Expeditionary Force sailed. Herbert Walker, the General Manager, said later that the Government had given him 60 hours to prepare 350 trains of 30 vehicles each to go to the Port. For several weeks a train arrived at the dockside every twelve minutes, fourteen hours a day. Thereafter the servicing of the Front and of the 176 camps on the system pressed heavily on normal services; also the provision of ambulance trains depleted carriage stock, and the Eastleigh Works was given over to war purposes, so that after the completion of the first batch of H15 4-6-0s in 1914, no new engines were built for six years.

After 1918, the slow run-down of the port activity and the camps inhibited plans for new civilian services for many months; however the L&SWR was fortunate in that it already had proved prototypes of better carriages and more powerful engines, so that by the time the 'Grouping' came along it was in better shape than its two partners, and was to be the main revenue-provider and senior partner in things mechanical. As regards the Southampton line however, there was some shift of emphasis. Higher wages and longer holidays meant that seaside travel was booming, and the Company realised that in the unspoilt beaches of the far West it had a great asset. The best engines and stock began to be put on the trains proceeding west of Exeter, and in 1926 the full weight of publicity was put behind the new 'Atlantic Coast Express'. The Bournemouth line received less attention and did not have a named train until the 'Bournemouth Belle' was put on in 1931, an all-Pullman train which from 9 September ran on Sundays only in Winter until 1 January 1936 when it became daily, doing the trip in Summer in two hours flat.

In 1932 it was decided that the Royal Agricultural Show should be held at Stoneham Park, three miles from Eastleigh. In those days it was assumed that most of the exhibition material and livestock would travel by rail (the previous year the GWR had built a new station for it at Warwick) and it was up to the SR to pull out all the stops. It was decided to build a new dock for the cattle at the Cheesemarket in Eastleigh sidings, and to work the haulage of machinery from Bevois Park Siding, Southampton. The East Yard at Eastleigh was extended, but this was not enough, and the so-called Ammunition Sidings had to be used as well. The traffic normally using this siding was diverted to some refurbished old sidings near Micheldever. The road transport required to forward all the loads on to Stoneham Park was also considerable, and a wide corduroy road of sleepers had to be laid right through the Carriage Works.

Southampton West station about 1904, with a Great Western train in the Up platform.

Bournemouth express passing Surbiton about 1914; T14 class 'Paddlebox' 4-6-0 No. 443.

Up Bournemouth train with H15 class 4-6-0 near Farnborough on 31 August 1934 (R.W. Kidner).

Pick-up goods with T3 class 4-4-0 No. 557 near Farnborough on 21 August 1934 (R.W. Kidner).

A long Down goods train with S15 class 4-6-0 No. 507 near Hook on 17 May 1936 (R.W. Kidner).

An Up Ocean Liner Express with H15 4-6-0 No. 476 near Basingstoke on 15 May 1937 (R.W. Kidner).

In the early thirties the line was at its busiest at the London end, mainly due to the increase in frequency of suburban services. The average allowance of time between trains was 4 minutes, and the only way to keep everything moving fast enough to avoid delays to the main line trains was to reduce this to 2½ minutes. It was proposed to build a new fly-over at Durnsford Road (Wimbledon) to bring the trains from local stations such as Kingston and Hampton Court off the then Up lines and over to the Down side for easier running into Waterloo. This work was begun in 1935, and brought about the following changes: Down through became Up local, Up through became Down through, Up local became Up through; the Up main local flew over the Up through and Down through. This required alterations also at Vauxhall, and the station was closed for a time, re-opening on 9 March 1936. The Down main local platform was replaced by a new island platform between the Down main local and new Up main local, thus providing a platform face for all lines.

Much work was also done at the Southampton end, apart from Docks work described elsewhere. Southampton Central station was rebuilt, the old Up main becoming Up local, the old Down an island between the through lines, and a new Down platform being built with a Down bay at the west end. At the same time Blechynden level crossing was abolished and the line four-tracked to Millbrook.

Colour-light signalling came later to the Western Section than to the others; however, on 17 May 1936 it was inaugurated from Vauxhall to Malden, and next year to Woking. The complex tracks between Vauxhall and Waterloo were dealt with in October 1936. Thirty years later the country portion of the line was given these signals, the work being completed in sections: Woking to Farnborough 5 June 1966, Northam Junction area 2 October, Worting Junction to St. Denys 12 November, Brookwood to Worting 19 November; the section through Southampton Central to Brockenhurst came into use on 22 October.

On 4 July 1937, the Portsmouth line was electrified; electric services now extended down the Southampton line as far as Woking, and a spin-off was that a number of 'Schools' class 4-4-0s became available, adding to the number of Maunsell classes to be seen on the line, and more of the modern carriage stock could be rostered for the Bournemouth line.

Summer Sundays were very busy days on the line in the 'thirties. Since most people then worked on Saturdays, excursions tended to run on the Sunday. These came from many places on and off the SR. However the booked service was also heavy, with many reliefs having to be run. On an evening visit to the line south of Woking on Sunday 2 September 1934, the author noted the following succession of Up trains, showing both Up lines used to the full (passing times):

10.0 12 coaches, slow line	10.6 9 coaches, slow line
10.1 11 coaches, fast line	10.8 12 coaches, fast line
10.4 14 coaches, slow line	10.10 Van train, slow line
10.5 12 coaches, fast line.	

From the outbreak of War in 1939, the Southampton line again became of prime national importance. Leave trains for the BEF were run from October that year. The Southern fitted out two complete ambulance trains, and these ran daily from Southampton Docks via Winchester Chesil on to the DNSR to army depots on Salisbury Plain and in the Midlands. The build-up for the Normandy invasion was a particularly testing time. Many of the largest ammunition dumps were in the DNSR area and this traffic put extra strain on the line south of Shawford. There was a large transit camp at Eastleigh which received trains of all companies' stock running via Kensington or Reading; in addition there was the massive traffic to the Docks. During 1944 there was a nightly train from Waterloo including two LNER sleeping cars, for VIP traffic; it is said that when General Eisenhower or Montgomery went that way the 'Royal Engine,' T9 No. 119, was used.

After the War, things return to normal slowly; the winding down of the British and US Forces took time. The building programme of 'Merchant Navy' and 'Battle of Britain' Pacifics allowed more of the better engines to be allocated to the Bournemouth line, and new carriages to Bulleid's design caused the final removal of old L&SWR stock. On 26 November 1947 in darkness under the automatic signal gantries, near Farnborough, there was a serious accident. The 3.5 pm from Bournemouth with 'Lord Nelson' Class No. 860 was waiting at signal No. WA113 which had failed. The driver was unable to make contact with Farnborough box. Meanwhile the 12.15 from Ilfracombe was allowed into the section by the signalman at Fleet. This train, with *King Arthur* at the head ran into the rear of the stationary train; a passenger and a railway servant were killed; the Fleet signalman was held responsible, for not establishing block working.

ALL CHANGE: 1949 onwards

The first few years of nationalisation were optimistic and exciting. 'Britannia' and 'Merchant Navy' Pacifics made a fine sight on the 'Belle' and the experiments with differing liveries for coaching stock, carried out on the Bournemouth line as on some others, provided variety at least, though none received enthusiastic support and the many green carriages still running looked more fitting. However, there was no denying that holidaymakers were turning to cars and much freight passing to the road. Many familiar types of engine, after briefly carrying the horrible block-lettering 'British Railways' on their tenders, went from the scene. Soon even 'King Arthurs' were not too clean and punctuality declined. Sometimes it was not the railway's fault; there was a big earth-slip of the embankment between Hook and Winchfield in January 1961, two tracks being out of use for several weeks. Some trains ran via Alton, some via Portsmouth, and others by way of Hounslow or Richmond and Wokingham over the GWR from Reading to Basingstoke.

Meanwhile the abolition of steam was proceeding with indecent haste. The plan for the Bournemouth line was to go straight from steam to electric, but in fact there was a short partial diesel era. Passengers on the local services who had their eyes not on their newspapers were surprised to see class 33 diesel-electrics attached to eight-coach trains apparently running backwards. This novel method had been proved with lengthy trials on the Oxted line with a demotored Portsmouth EMU, and also between Ashford and Headcorn at speeds up to 100 mph. The exact form of the new interchangeable tractor units and trailer units is described later.

Although some steam engines were still giving sparkling performances, there were exceptions, as on 29 December 1966 when 'Merchant Navy' No. 34077 lost power near Woking, and from Farnborough had to be assisted by diesel-electric No. D6549. From January 1967 even the 'Belle' was diesel-hauled at times, including the very last working.

The electric current was switched on to Southampton in December 1966 and many test trains ran. A partial public service commenced as far as Basingstoke on 2 January 1967 and to Bournemouth on 3 April. A foretaste of what was to come was given by scheduling the 0656 to Waterloo to leave 19 minutes later and arrive three minutes earlier. It had been intended to start the full service in June, but much of the new stock was late in arriving and it did not start until 10 July. The face of the Southampton line was now changing rapidly; the 'Belle' and 'Royal Wessex' went, also many goods facilities. The Micheldever (Weston) loops closed in 1966, although electric lines had been laid; Winchester Goods went in 1969 and Woking Goods in 1970. The old Terminus station closed, together with Northam, on 7 March 1966, and even the well-known clock-tower at Central station went down. However, the Channel Islands trains continued to run (but to Weymouth) and some Ocean Liner trains still wended their way past the derelict Terminus and across Canute Road.

The changes were not all destructive; the new colour-light signalling system was centred on Eastleigh and a new box at the London end was opened in November 1966, controlling all trains between St. Denys and Worting Junction. At the same time Eastleigh acquired a new diesel depot. Extra traffic was brought to the area with the opening of a coal concentration depot at Dibbles Wharf, Northam. The operators purchased a B4 0-4-0T, BR 30096, and renamed her *Corrall Queen*. Working trains from Northam sidings to the wharf, this engine crossed a busy public road and became a well-known sight, so that when laid aside she was 'preserved'.

The new trains proved to have a good turn of speed. In June 1968 after a letter appeared in 'The Railway Magazine' extolling three 'end of steam' runs with 'Merchant Navy' engines, all of which hit the 100 mph between Hook and Bramshot, another correspondent wrote to point out that on 22 October 1967 travelling in a train comprising one REP 'tractor unit' and one 4-TC trainer unit, he had reached the hundred just after Hook (Up direction), held it to Fleet reaching a maximum of 107 mph, and hit 100 again at Brookwood.

The impressive outline of rebuilt 'Merchant Navy' Pacific No. 35022 heading the 'Bournemouth Belle' at Waterloo in 1956 (R.W. Kidner).

GWR No. 3440 'City of Truro' restored for preservation, in temporary service at Southampton Terminus on 23 May 1957 on a Newbury train (H.C. Casserley).

A table of Southern Region trains booked between stops at over 60 mph put out in 1967 was headed by thirteen trains between Basingstoke and Woking at 72.19 mph, two the other way at 70.38 and twelve at 68.42; one run from Winchester to Waterloo at 69.48, eight from Waterloo to Southampton at 67.93 and six the other way at 67.91. The voltage in the electric rail between Waterloo and Brookwood was the normal 660, but this was then increased in 25 volt stages to 750V, giving every chance for very fast running at the country end.

The Royal Family had their first taste of the new regimen on 7 August 1967, when their train to join the Royal Yacht ran behind 'Warship' class diesel D819, taking the curve at Millbrook into the West (New) Docks.

In April 1970 there were considerable track alterations at Northam Junction, in the course of which the line to the Eastern Docks was singled. During the work Bournemouth trains were diverted via Romsey from Eastleigh, and this now freight-only line saw such exciting trains as 12-coach 'electrics' propelled by two Class 33 diesel-electrics.

There is little further to be said: the electric service has continued to provide speed and comfort which would have been unimaginable in the first fifty years of the line's history. Railway interest has of course suffered, though the continuing Boat Trains and cross-country locomotive-hauled trains provide some variety. Gone are the untidy mixed goods trains, and strange forms of wagon in block formation have taken their place. All in all, 145 years after it opened, the Southampton line is not in bad shape.

THE ROUTE DESCRIBED

The history of Waterloo station itself has been described in the text; its present condition derives mainly from the rebuilding of 1909 onwards, and at this vast terminus the Southampton trains normally departed from the platforms immediately south of what is still a fairly distinct 'Windsor lines side'. The first few hundred yards of track pursue a somewhat sinuous course, which made even a level start quite hard work for the locomotive, due to the increased friction. It is still a very busy track; in steam days the working of light engines to and from Nine Elms and Clapham Junction had to be added to the already heavy passenger traffic occupation, and they were often worked in groups of up to five coupled together to minimise this problem.

The first station, Vauxhall, seems to most passengers just a place one runs through, but it has an interesting history. Not least, perhaps, that it is said to have given its name to the Russian word for railway station (Vokshal in our script); this arose from a visit by the then Czar who was charmed by the Vauxhall Gardens, the 'pleasurama' of the late eighteenth century, which was a favourite haunt up to its closing in 1859, and he built a replica in Russia complete with a railway station. However, it seems probable that this was based on the Nine Elms terminus, then often referred to as Vauxhall, and not the present station on the 'Metropolitan Extension'. This had four tracks when opened, and so remained until 1884, when two more tracks were added and most of the later station built. Meanwhile, road traffic underneath it was building up, including horse-trams, and the road junctions at each end of the underbridge were becoming congested. When in 1898 the L&SWR asked for two more tracks and another platform, it was pointed out that this would convert the underbridge into more of a tunnel. However, it was done, and this gloomy cavern was to see many millions of frustrated motorists and tramdrivers waiting impatiently to emerge from the traffic jams into daylight. In 1935, yet another platform was added, making eight. An unusual feature was that all roads had delivery points down which milk tank wagons could discharge to the Creamery below, this having been for many years a destination for milk trains working up from the pastures of the West. In practice, most of this comprised short rakes of tankers worked from Clapham Junction and stood on the Up Windsor Slow. The Nine Elms goods station on the Up side, now covered by the new Covent Garden market, was a busy place and notable in the 'thirties for the ancient Beyer Peacock 0-6-0ST engines which shunted there. Queen Victoria's private station had been there, but was closed by 1900. The goods depot closed in 1968. Nine Elms locomotive shed, on the opposite side of the main line, closed in 1967.

We now approach a large area of trackwork knitting; passing over the original low-level lines by which the LBSC and LCDR approached Victoria, we see Queens Road station sandwiched under the girders of the high-level lines of the two companies which replaced them in the 'sixties. On the Down side is Longhedge Junction, where the lines from Victoria and from Brixton fed into the West London Extension Railway, as well as the site of the Longhedge LCDR locomotive works and the later Stewarts Lane depot. On the Up side there was the South Lambeth goods depot of the GWR, approached over LBSC metals. At West London Junction the embankment of the former line from Kensington into Waterloo is somewhat obscured; here also were several carriage sidings, with a later train-washing plant. We pass over the WLER line from Longhedge to Kensington and the LCDR line from Brixton to Clapham Junction (Richmond side), and shortly after over the WLER line to the LBSC side of Clapham Junction. The ex-LBSC main line runs beside us, but there was no junction, apart from a common exchange siding between the two main lines.

Clapham Junction is now an amalgam of three stations; the L&SWR one was built around the fork of the Richmond and Main lines, with the LBSC one lying to the south, and a small WLER presence south of that; the L&SWR trains over the WLER used the Richmond lines platforms. Carriage sidings were built over the space within the fork. The LSW side was extensively rebuilt around 1905, with a wide overhead walkway right across it and leading up to the road bridge at its south end. Subsequently, the LBSC side was also rebuilt, and in SR days a new entrance to the whole station was constructed at the north end of the bridge; the old entrance was closed and

The Southampton line platforms at Clapham Junction about 1903, showing the old station building, and an M7 0-4-4T on a local train.

The same viewpoint in 1905, showing the new station and overhead walkways; Adams 'Jubilee' 0-4-2 with a 'bogie block' train. On right, LBSC Down platform, and goods train coming off the West London Extension line.

the hall leading from it to the L&SWR walkway became a signalling school. As the LSW main line passes under the road bridge, the ex-LBSC line swings away to the south.

Wimbledon was a major station, and exchange point with the District Railway trains running north to Earls Court (on SR metals as far as East Putney) and the trains running east over the joint LSW–LBSC Tooting loop; also after 1930 over the new line to Sutton. The station was entirely reconstructed in 1929, with the former LBSC station abolished. A large engineering works complex on the Down side, Down end, always contained a fascinating collection of service vehicles; on the Up side, Down end, there was a milk depot with its own siding. The tracks here are shared by a number of services, but the flying junctions at Raynes Park, Malden and Surbiton mitigated crossing delays; yet another one west of Weybridge took traffic from the Windsor area running towards Woking. That station, the junction for the Guildford line, the most important so far, was a busy place with a large p.w. yard as well as extensive goods sidings. The large L&SWR orphanage, opened in 1909, was built on $7\frac{1}{2}$ acres of land purchased from the London Necropolis Co. At Brookwood, there were two minor junctions, one to Bisley Camp and the other to Necropolis. The former only saw much traffic during the summer target-shooting weeks on the range, though in the 1914–18 War, when the branch was extended through Pirbright to Blackdown Camp, it handled much military traffic. The Necropolis branch was in regular use from 1854 to 1941 (when its London station was bombed out); the trains were short and comprised one or more coffin vans with compos for mourners; in 1864, a station was built at Brookwood on the main line, paid for by the Necropolis Company, for the convenience of mourners and others not travelling on the coffin train. Before passing under the flying junction with the Alton line, there is a magnificent stretch of deep but wide cutting: Deepcut.

Out in the open again, the old Basingstoke Canal can be seen parelleling the railway on its north side, and just before Pirbright Junction this turns south, crossing the main line on an aqueduct, which as befits the weight of water above, is carried on heavy arches, one for each track. The Pirbright junctions are complex, and formerly included a line running from the LSW on the Up side to join the SE&CR Reading line; both companies had stations in Farnborough. We are now in long-time Army territory; to the south lies Laffan's Plain and Aldershot's Long Valley. We cross the large Fleet Pond and come to Basingstoke; from here a light railway formerly branched off to Alton, and west of the station there was also a short branch to Park Prewett Hospital. This was also the point at which the Great Western line from Reading joined, and both companies had engine sheds, the L&SWR one being opened in 1905. The GWR station lay to the north, and no physical connection was possible until mixed gauge was laid in 1856. In 1932, this station was partly absorbed into a rebuilt SR station; however the separate GWR loco shed remained in use until 1950.

The cutting at Deepcut dwarfing a local train with M7 class 0-4-4T, 31 August 1934 (R.W. Kidner).

The Basingstoke Canal aqueduct near Farnborough on 18 August 1934; top, from the lineside, below from the canal (R.W. Kidner).

The layout of the Worting Junction flyover has already been described. After the Exeter line has departed there is a long station-less stretch of ten miles, double track only, with some fairly heavy engineering comprising the short Litchfield Tunnel (near the 'summit') and the twin Popham Tunnels. Micheldever was for many years a four-track station. North of here there are large excavations of chalk, some of which was used to build up the West Docks at Southampton, and various sidings have existed, in which in the 'thirties lines of condemned or dubious carriage stock could be observed. The Weston loops were followed by Wallers Ash Tunnel, and at Winchester Junction a further line from Alton came in, the junction facing south. The line now passed over the Didcot, Newbury & Southampton Railway; at this point from 1943 to 1951 there was a single line spur from Worthy Down for Up trains only. Winchester station was renamed City in 1949 to differentiate it from the Chesil or Cheesehill station of the DNSR, but reverted to plain Winchester when the latter was closed (for regular trains 1960, all trains 1966). The L&SWR station embodied a large goods depot which was approached by a severe curve, necessitating the use of 0-4-0T shunters; from 1927 this engine was housed here in a sub-shed. Two miles south of the station came Shawford Junction, where the GWR trains via the DN&SR came on to the Southampton line. Through Shawford station, and alongside the River Itchen, we come to Eastleigh, running over a short four-track section. Apart from its importance as a junction with the Romsey and Fareham lines, this area had its future drastically altered by the decision in 1908 to close down the Nine Elms locomotive works and to move all engine and carriage construction to a new site at Eastleigh in the angle between the main and Fareham lines, where carriage construction had been carried out since 1890. The works was progressively enlarged until it covered 81 acres; in Southern days the closure of Brighton Works brought much more work to Eastleigh. It is now classed as a BR Engineering Ltd. depot, with a by-pass line from the north of the station and a loop round the south of the depot. Eastleigh locomotive shed was opened in 1903, displacing Northam as the main shed.

South of Eastleigh proper, where the present Southampton Airport station is placed, there was in the 'twenties a platform on the Down line only, named 'Atlantic Park Hostel Halt'; this served a camp for immigrants to the USA.

At Swaythling we are well into the modern Southampton connurbation; the next station, St. Denys, is an awkward one, with platforms on both the main and Portsmouth line. Immediately afterwards lines branched off on the Down side to Mount Pleasant sidings and on the Up to Bevois Park yard. At Northam Junction the Bournemouth line swung west through the 528-yard Southampton Tunnel. Northam station was inside the triangle which formed by that line, the Terminus-to-West spur, and the main line which went straight on. Northam had a locomotive shed serving Southampton until 1903 when Eastleigh shed took over the duties. Northam station was closed in 1966 as it had platforms only on the Terminus line. The Terminus

The Micheldever carriage sidings in 1953, looking towards Popham Tunnel No. 2 (RHC: Collection H.C. Casserley).

A D15 class 4-4-0 No. 471 working Ocean Liner Pullmans to Southampton, near Hook on 17 May 1936 (R.W. Kidner).

Eastleigh Works on 8 April 1932 (R.W. Kidner).

Eastleigh Works on 14 May 1981; Weymouth to Waterloo train with REP set 3013 leading (J. Scrace).

station had a six-platform layout with overall roof. From the point where the station lines swung west, the tracks leading straight on went to a large goods depot, and across Canute Road to the Docks. The build-up of the docks lines is covered elsewhere; all were rail-served.

TRAIN SERVICES

The early services have already been described. There were no dramatic changes in the next twenty years, and in 1861 there were only nine trains a day from Southampton to London, taking from 2 hours 20 minutes to 3 hours. Full use was made of the fast trains; the 8.40 from Docks joined up with or connected with the 6.25 from Weymouth, then at Eastleigh with the 7.55 from Salisbury and the 8.0 from Portsmouth, the whole arriving at Waterloo at 11.0. Even more of a 'catch-all' train was the 11.30 from Docks, which picked up from all-stations trains from Weymouth, Salisbury, Portsmouth and Alton, and at Basingstoke took on passengers off the 7.35 from Exeter for intermediate stations into London, as that train ran non-stop from here. For the cheap passenger, the going was really slow; the 12.30 'Govt' took four hours. However, the L&SWR was praised by commentators for allowing 3rd class passengers on more of their trains than most railways.

The service on the Southampton line might have remained in the doldrums had it not been for stirrings in Bournemouth. The leading lights in this rising town had been lobbying hard for a direct line from London, using the Great Western interest in the DN&SR proposals as a lever. When in 1888 the L&SWR finally opened their direct line via Sway, the Company was in honour bound to give a good service. The Chairman had been hinting at Bournemouth in 2¼ hours, and the resulting accelerations gave Southampton a better service, albeit that the focus was shifted from the Terminus to West station.

The Locomotive Department made its contribution by providing four new classes of 4-4-0, two with 7 ft. 1 in. driving wheels; though it was a T3 with 6 ft. 7 in. driving wheels that made two remarkable runs on 8 March 1897 on the 10 a.m. Down and 5 p.m. Up between Waterloo and Bournemouth in 124 minutes each way. To please the new prosperous visitors to that resort, Pullmans were put on certain trains from 1900, though from 1906 to 1908 these were phased out and replaced by Eastleigh-built dining cars. The Drummond 4-cylinder 4-6-0s when they arrived, though not perhaps meeting all expectations, did allow even faster running with heavier loads, and by 3 July 1911 the timetables showed Southampton reached in 100 minutes and Bournemouth (non-stop) in 2 hours. This was well within capacity; No. 462 with ten carriages ran to Southampton in 1911 in 84½ minutes.

The outbreak of War in August 1914 caused alterations to the timetables to provide paths for the large number of troop and supply trains needed for the Front; the boat service to Cherbourg was cancelled, though sailings to Le Havre and St. Malo continued. There were further more severe cuts in 1917. The War had come at a time when the railway was poised for even better things, with improved 4-6-0 engines and a new style of carriage. During the conflict and for some time after, capacity rather than speed was the thing, and when normal conditions returned and the new engines and stock were being turned out again, the emphasis had shifted somewhat to the Exeter line.

Under the Southern Railway aegis, some attention was paid to the Bournemouth traffic, and on 8 July 1929 a 'Bournemouth Limited' was introduced, taking 2 hours flat with no stop at Southampton. However the following 4.45 p.m. was not a bad train for Southampton, taking 89 minutes. The tables showed two trains per week calling at Bramshot Golf Club Halt for members only; both were on Sunday, and timing ensured that everyone had to stay at the Club for lunch. As was usual with the SR, there were plenty of oddities: a 12.5 a.m. from Waterloo to Farnborough on Wednesdays, and a 12.0 midnight to Winchester on Thursdays; also on Wednesdays and Saturdays a through train from Eastleigh at 11.2 p.m. to Lymington. At that time most lines had their mail train; that on the Southampton line was the 9.50 p.m. from Weymouth. It was not fast; after arriving at Southampton West at 12.27 a.m., it did not leave Docks until 1.10; however, a night reveller could pick it up at Surbiton at 3.33 a.m. Usually only one passenger carriage was attached, and dozing was only possible between stops as the mail vans were detached and attached without ceremony.

On 5 July 1931 the all-Pullman 'Bournemouth Belle' was introduced, originally intended as a summer-only train, but kept on for Winter Sundays, and made daily from 1 January 1936; by the summer it was doing the Up run in 2 hours. For the inaugural run of the 'Bournemouth Belle' *Lord Nelson* had been rostered, but for some reason was unavailable, so E780 *Sir Persant* took over. It was not a brilliant run, taking 95 minutes to Southampton with ten Pullman cars; there were no fewer than five signal checks, due to several National Sunday League excursions being in front. The return journey was better, 86 minutes. A dead stand at St. Denys meant that *Sir Persant* had to make up time, and managed the last 70 miles in just under 70 minutes in spite of some slowing on the pull up to Litchfield summit. The best speed was 77.9 mph between mileposts 25 and 20.

In general, running seems to have mostly been as good or better than the timetable. Mr. Frank Box, a well-known West Country railway enthusiast, timed many trains and study of his charts suggest that the three main types of engine in use in the late 'thirties all did equally well. Several runs in 1939 showed maximum speeds as follows:

'Lord Nelson' Class 865, 71½ mph at Byfleet, with 10 Pullmans
'Lord Nelson' Class 852, 72 mph at Shawford, with 12 Pullmans
'King Arthur' Class 779, 75 mph at Micheldever, with 12 Pullmans
'Schools' Class 924, 78 mph at Shawford, with 12 coaches.

The Down 'Bournemouth Belle' with 'Lord Nelson' 4-6-0 No. 856 near Basingstoke on 15 May 1937 (R.W. Kidner).

The Worting flyover on 31 August 1934; an Up Southampton semi-fast is passing over the Exeter line (R.W. Kidner).

Class 5 4-6-0 No. 73088 on a Down Southampton train at Winchester City, 27 August 1963 (J. Scrace).

'Merchant Navy' 4-6-2 No. 35024 on a Bournemouth train at Winchester; on the left is the B4 class 0-4-0T No. 30102 used to shunt the City Goods Depot; 20 September 1962 (J. Scrace).

These were all Down runs; in the Up direction speeds were a little higher, 'Lord Nelson' class 865 reaching 80 mph at Brookwood, and 'Schools' class 924 reaching 79½ mph at Byfleet.

The cross-Channel services remained popular and in 1931 the service to St. Malo became non-tidal.

The era of the big flying-boats, based in the Solent, was now dawning, and in 1937 a service was put on for passengers using the Empire Flying Boats of Imperial Airways. Initially, two Pullmans and a van were added to the 8.30 a.m. from Waterloo and detached at Southampton Central. Later special trains were run, but from Victoria which was closer to the air terminal, joining the main line at Wimbledon. The Southampton terminal was at berth 50, between the Ocean Dock and the Town Quay. These trains were continued during the War, but the destination was Poole. After the War the Southampton terminal was re-opened and the service lasted into the 'fifties, when the flying-boats were phased out.

Another innovation on 22 July 1939 was a day-time service to St. Malo leaving Waterloo at 8.15 a.m. on Thursdays and Saturdays. There was also a day service to Le Havre.

There was little change until the outbreak of War, when many services were cancelled, but most later restored. There was very heavy pressure from service trains initially, until Dunkirk. Then from 1943, troop trains again led to a shortage of paths, locos and stock for civilian trains. Many of these trains terminated at Eastleigh, for the transit camp, troops being trucked to the Docks. After the War, the pattern returned to normal, but as cars became available, the number of weekend excursion trains and relief workings was reduced.

The SR managed to restore two Bournemouth non-stops in 1946, but they ran on Saturdays only (9.20 a.m. and 2.30 p.m. from Waterloo); their timing, 141 and 138 minutes, was not impressive. The truth was that there was now little public interest in chipping minutes off services; the passengers were apathetic, and the management no longer anxious to give a sparkling image. By winter 1956 there was a service to Bournemouth from Waterloo at the half-hours most hours, reaching there in 2 hours 10 minutes (the 'Belle') to 3 hours. The 'Royal Wessex' (4.35 p.m. from Waterloo) whose main interest was a through portion to Swanage, was not a fast train; it took 1 hour 33 minutes to Southampton and 2 hours 20 minutes to Bournemouth Central. An interesting service was the 9 p.m. from Waterloo to Southampton Terminus, which was advertised to run to Docks in summer and on some days in the winter; it was given three extra minutes on these occasions. This was in fact the vestige of the Channel Islands service; it was now summer weekdays only, with an extra train on Fridays and Saturdays. The Le Havre boat train now ran only on Mondays, Wednesdays and Fridays outwards, and was discontinued entirely after 8 May 1964. Channel Islands services were transferred to Weymouth on 13 May 1961.

After electrification, the basic service was a non-stop to Southampton at 30 minutes past most hours, reaching Southampton in 1 hour 10 minutes and

Bournemouth in 1 hour 40 minutes; and a semi-fast at 41 minutes past the hour taking 1 hour 26 minutes to Southampton and 2 hours 7 minutes to Bournemouth. The 'newspaper' train (02.45) now took 2 hours 39 minutes to Bournemouth, and there were still a few oddities beloved of Southern time-tablers, such as the 00.02 from Eastleigh to Southampton on Mondays only, and the 00.07 from St. Denys to Southampton which was Mondays Excepted. "Ah," you will say, "Of course the 00.02 did the St. Denys stop on a Monday" — but in fact it did not. The 00.08 Up from Christchurch took $3\frac{1}{2}$ hours to reach Waterloo — and only stopped at Farnborough on Mondays! The 1974 tables offered 22 trains per day to Bournemouth from Waterloo (24 on summer Saturdays). Workings from Bournemouth to the Midlands and North were on the whole generous: on weekdays one covering Sheffield, York, Newcastle, Leeds and Birmingham, and another covering Birmingham and Liverpool: on summer Saturdays, one to Birmingham and Manchester, two to Sheffield, Birmingham and Leeds, two to Birmingham and Liverpool, one to Sheffield, York and Newcastle — six trains per day to Birmingham from Bournemouth, seven from Southampton. The current tables are very similar, except that the fast leaves at 35 minutes past the hour and has clipped 3 minutes off the time to Southampton and 4 minutes off Bournemouth. The semi-fast leaves at 46 minutes past the hour and is 2 minutes faster to both.

Ocean Liner trains still use the Canute Road crossing on occasion, but they proceed to the new Queen Elizabeth II Terminal, not the 1950 Ocean Terminal. Others use the Millbrook loop to reach berths 105/6 in the West Docks.

Finally, mention must be made of services over the Southampton line coming from outside the L&SWR system. A complete history of these would be very complex, since few were maintained or followed the same route for very long; the following notes are therefore not exhaustive.

From 1893 a through carriage from Sheffield ran via the Midland & South Western Junction Railway to Andover and to Southampton via Eastleigh. A carriage from Bradford was also worked two days a week, being added to the 'American and Cape Lines Express' from Cheltenham. Shortly afterwards the 'North' and 'South' expresses were instituted, running to Southampton from Sheffield, Leeds and Manchester in various years; however, all ceased in 1914, though a through service from Liverpool was re-instituted in 1921 and ran until 1939.

The Didcot, Newbury & Southampton line was used for through coaches from Leicester via GCR from 1901, and a through train from Newcastle ran from 1903. It ran in most years until 1939 and at times included through coaches from Glasgow and Scarborough. However, most trains from the GCR ran via Reading and Basingstoke, from Birkenhead from 1903, Manchester 1910, and in some years Bradford, Huddersfield, Leeds and Nottingham. Services ceased in 1939, but were restored after the War from Newcastle, York and Derby.

The former LC&DR link between Farringdon St. (Widened Lines) and

N class 2-6-0 No. 31873 on a Down van train at Winchester, 25 May 1965 (J. Scrace).

Winchester to Bournemouth train at Eastleigh on 14 May 1981; VEP set No. 7712 (J. Scrace).

St. Denys on 18 April 1981; TC unit 406 leading a Bournemouth train (J. Scrace).

Class 33 No. 6553 crossing Canute Road, Southampton, on 20 July 1970 (J. Scrace).

Clapham Junction was used from 1905 to 1910 for a service from various GNR stations to Bournemouth.

The West London Railway route from Willesden to Clapham Junction was used for through trains off the LNWR from 1905 (Liverpool) and 1922/3 from Aberdeen and Glasgow to Southampton Docks. A service from Coventry to Bournemouth ran this way in 1929–33.

That cross-country services remained popular, especially with holiday-makers having a lot of luggage and children, is proved by the fact that in 1968 for instance, there were three trains on weekdays from Southampton, covering Birmingham Sheffield and York; five on winter Saturdays covering also Bradford; and seven on summer Saturdays, bringing in also Leeds, Wolverhampton and Manchester.

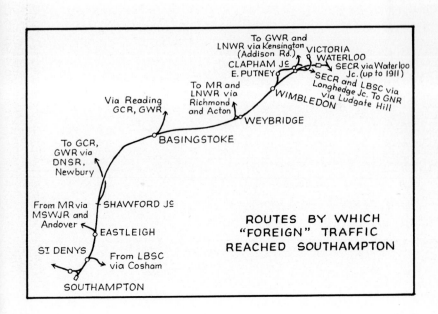

ROUTES BY WHICH
"FOREIGN" TRAFFIC
REACHED SOUTHAMPTON

A through Birmingham–Bournemouth train at Basingstoke; the engine is a
de Glehn compound 4-4-2 No. 102 'La France' (P.V. Williams).

A train of LMS mail-vans leaving Eastleigh, with S11 class 4-4-0 No. E404 on
7 July 1926; note 'special' headboard at nearside buffer (H.C. Casserley).

THE DOCKS

It goes without saying that the history of Southampton as a maritime centre would fill several volumes; it was used by the Phoenicians and Romans, and lately archaeologists have made interesting discoveries of pre-Saxon and Saxon times in the tongue between the River Itchin and the River Test. The scouring action of these rivers gives a six-mile deep haven — 'Southampton Water' — and it was natural that in due course ocean-going ships would seek to use it. By 1803, Harbour Commissioners had been appointed, the Town Quay and Royal Victoria Pier were built in 1831, and in 1843 the Outer Dock was dug out. The Inner Dock (locked) followed in 1851, the Itchen Quays 1876, Graving Dock 1879, Empress Dock 1890, Test South Quays 1902, Trafalgar Graving Dock 1905, White Star Dock (later Ocean Dock) 1911, Floating Dock 1924. Developments were dictated by the decisions of the large liner operators to move in, and by their building larger and larger vessels. All the docks were rail-served, with a network of lines stemming from near the old Terminus station and running across Canute Road. In January 1891 the L&SWR opened a station at the Royal Pier, served by trains via Terminus — though special condensing engines had to be attached for the trip through the streets.

On 1 November 1892, the L&SWR bought the Port. Undoubtedly this was a wise decision. Under railway management they became extremely prosperous, and competitive. For example, imported meat off the ships was packed into horse-carts which were then dispatched to London on trains of flat-wagons, ready to roll off on to the streets without further delay. A prized traffic was bullion from South Africa. This was sent to Waterloo usually on passenger trains in a specially-strengthened bogie parcels van with asphalt flooring. When there was a large consignment a special train was made up, and on occasion such a train could be carrying one million pounds worth of specie.

During the 1914–18 War, the docks were virtually closed to civilian traffic. The tonnages of equipment and numbers of men shipped were colossal, even though in that war the shorter cross-Channel routes remained open. In 1917, a train-ferry berth was set up just west of the Royal Pier, with a swing-link giving a 12-foot tidal range. The vessel used was one of three built, two being used at Richborough Port in Kent. All were sold in 1924 to the LNER and moved to Harwich.

It was in 1929 that the Southern Railway began the biggest expansion plan in the Port's history. Since all the space in the old area was filled, it was necessary in effect to build some more land. A 2-mile quay wall was built northwards from the Royal Pier as far as Millbrook, and by using a network of railway lines, the marsh area behind it as far as the railway to Bournemouth was filled in with soil. By 1933, the King George V Graving Dock at the north end was opened, and the new ocean quays began to be

The White Star Dock (Ocean Dock) about 1920, probably taken from the roof of the South Western Hotel. Behind the long shed is a train of ready-packed London meat cars on flat-wagons. There are two docks shunters (a C14 and a B4) in the foreground; the docks locomotive shed is at bottom left.

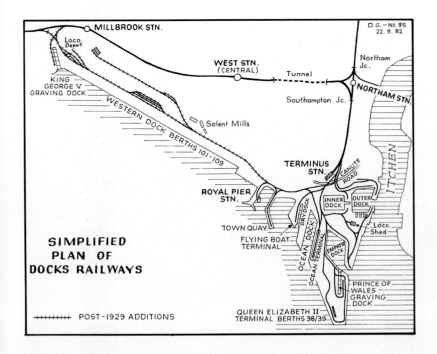

SIMPLIFIED
PLAN OF
DOCKS RAILWAYS

++++++ POST-1929 ADDITIONS

used. The SR had built a long loop line round the landward end from near Millbrook station, linking up with an extension of the Royal Pier line opened in 1929, and inside this loop much marine and industrial plant was put up, including the giant Spillers Flour Mill.

All kinds of traffic were encouraged; banana trains were handled with trains of special vans (in the first instance hired from the LNER, as the SR had no insulated vans); another trade was in South African crayfish—oddly enough, these were run through to Folkestone to cross the sea again to France, one train in 1933 taking 8,000 containers of crayfish.

On 31 July 1950, a new passenger and cargo terminal, the Ocean Terminal, was opened along the east side of the Ocean Dock at Southampton. This 1,000-foot-long building with a 100-foot tower at the seaward end had an island platform which could accommodate two full-length trains, and was linked to the ships by a light-alloy telescopic gangway. It was opened by the Prime Minister (Clement Attlee), who had travelled down in an all-Pullman train, headed by a 'Merchant Navy' class engine having a round headboard 'No. 1 Ocean Terminal Express'.

The Docks locomotive shed was located between Nos. 1 and 3 dry docks, south of Outer Dock. After the last War the situation where almost all traffic from any quay was rail-borne changed swiftly, and the requirement for

Ex-Lancashire & Yorkshire Railway 0-4-0ST (LMS 11243) as contractors' 'Bassett' filling in the land behind the West Quays near Millbrook on 8 April 1934 (R.W. Kidner).

Docks locomotives: top left, Shanks 0-4-0ST 'Cowes' in condensing form for working trains to the Royal Pier (Loco. Pub. Co.); top right, LSWR B4 0-4-0T 'Cherbourg' at berth 101 in the New Docks in 1934 (L.T. Catchpole); bottom left, 0-4-0ST 'Clausentum' E734 after moving to Guildford as shed pilot, in 1934 (F.L. Organ); bottom right, C14 class 0-4-0T shunting near the Town Quay in 1932 (R.W. Kidner).

GWR 2-6-0 No. 6347 crossing Canute Road in August 1934 to work the 7.10 p.m. goods from the Old Docks via M&SWJR. Note track to Town Quay left also policeman with red flag by engine (G.R. Wheeler).

Q1 class 0-6-0 No. 33021 by 'God's House Tower' about to enter No.5 Gate, working empty wagons to the Old Docks, September 1955 (G.R. Wheeler).

engine power was much less; however the shed remained in use until 1966. When the New Docks opened, a locomotive servicing bay was put in near the north-west exit of the loop line; it had a 65-foot turntable (later increased to 70 foot).

In recent years the history of the Port has been more of civic interest than railway, with roll-on ferries taking the vast amount of road traffic. However, the great New Docks scheme of the SR — of course not now railway-owned — continues to play its part in the diminishing regular liner traffic and the much-increased cruising liner scene.

The only considerable alterations in the Docks since the heyday of the SR are the abolition of the Inner Dock and the renaming of the Outer Dock 'Princess Alexandra Dock', and the setting up of the Queen Elizabeth II Terminal at the end of the spit jutting into the junction of the rivers Itchen and Test. West of the docks proper, the Millbrook Freightliner Terminal and Maritime Freightliner Terminal have been built, north and west of the Graving Dock. There are now 206 berths, the numbers starting in the Princess Alexandra Dock and running westwards. From 30 September 1979, there has been no rail connection between the East and West Docks.

LOCOMOTIVES

When the London & Southampton Railway opened, there were few locomotive builders, and those who had entered this new field had very little experience to call upon. Probably the directors had little choice other than to purchase four 2-2-0 engines by Bury, named *Lark, Hawk, Raven* and *Falcon*; similar engines were purchased by other lines, and all found them unsuited to passenger work. The L&S quickly changed to engines of the 2-2-2 type, which would oscillate less on the track, starting with *Southampton*, built by the Millbrook Foundry for a contractor, and then building up a stud from Vulcan Foundry and Tayleur, Sharp Roberts, and Rothwell. These engines with their 5 ft. 6 in. single driving wheels were fairly fast but not powerful. For goods work some 0-4-2 engines with 4 ft. 6 in. driving wheels were purchased. Locomotive affairs were at that time in the hands of a Joseph Woods, but in 1843 J.V. Gooch took over; he not only laid out a locomotive works across the line from Nine Elms station, but also began to dictate design, possibly helped by the Chief Engineer, Joseph Locke, rather than taking the builders' designs as they stood. The first four engines from Nine Elms, *Eagle, Hawk, Falcon* and *Vulture*, had 6 ft. 6 in. driving wheels, the largest so far on any standard gauge engine. Six-coupled wheels came with the *Bison, Buffalo, Elephant,* and *Rhinoceros* of 1844. The Works could not supply all the engines required, and many were purchased from outside makers; however, in 1849, just before Gooch retired to make way for Joseph Beattie, Nine Elms built the famous *Etna* (No. 118) with 7 ft. driving wheels, which was followed by seven similar engines in the next four

One of Adams's '445' class of engines which worked the Southampton expresses from 1883.

A Beattie standard goods engine of 1864, 'Mazeppa.'

years. According to a statement by Beattie in 1854, at that time some trains from Gosport, Salisbury and Southampton were joined together at Basingstoke and went forward as a train of up to 26 carriages. This would mean a load of about 120 tons, and one wonders if these 'singles' could handle this unaided. By 1859, there were coupled express engines at work, with 6 ft. driving wheels; however, 7 ft. singles continued to be built as well as further coupled engines.

This brief summary has not referred to the many tank engines built for local use, especially by William Beattie who took over in 1871, nor certain other types designed for other parts of the system. The first main line engines under W.G. Beattie's control (though no doubt ordered by his father) were the 273 class 0-6-0s; these were also the first of the 'modern' period in that some of them survived into the Southern Railway era, as did the following 302 class 0-6-0. However, that cannot be said of the revolutionary bogie express engine, the 348 class, which Beattie brought out in 1876. Probably because the boiler was not large enough for adequate steaming, they did not appeal to the next locomotive Superintendent, William Adams (1877) and only a few of the 20 survived the turn of the century. Adams's first express engine, the 135 class of 1880 only had 15 years or so in main-line use; he followed these with two more smallish classes of outside-cylinder 4-4-0, the 445 and 460 classes, which in later years were seldom seen east of Salisbury. However, his next class, the A12 0-4-2 of 1887, was numerous (90), long-lived, and seen all over the system. Adams had also started, in 1890, on his famous quartet of outside-cylinder 4-4-0s, the X2 and T6 with 7 ft. 1 in. driving wheels, and the T3 and X6 with 6 ft. 7 in. driving wheels; thus began the practice of having a 'small-wheeled' version of passenger express engines to suit the gradients west of Salisbury.

Meanwhile, the two standard goods 0-6-0 engines which were to hold sway all through the Southern era, had arrived, the 395 class of 1881 and the 700 class of 1897, the latter now in the era of Dugald Drummond, who took over in 1895; the latter class were also in due course rebuilt by Urie with superheaters.

Drummond's first attempt at an express engine for the Bournemouth line, though novel, was not a success. It was a 4-2-2-0, with four high-pressure cylinders driving each axle in pairs; only six were built. A similar class but without the uncoupled axles, the C8 of 1898, was not highly rated either. It was the next design, the T9, which hit the right note. A total of 66 were built from 1899 to 1901, with minor differences in batches; known as the 'Greyhounds', they were all superheated in due course and served not only all over the L&SWR, but later all over the SR, many into the late 'fifties.

Next came two classes often confused; the K10 which was virtually a small-wheeled version of the C8, and the L11, a small-wheeled version of the T9. These were classed as mixed traffic engines, with their 5 ft. 7 ins. driving wheels; though mostly fitted with six-wheeled tenders, some acquired the inside-bearing 4,000-gallon bogie tenders which were such a distinctive feature of Drummond designs. Though small-wheeled, they

The 10.30 a.m. Waterloo to Weymouth passing Wimbledon on 1 July 1899; T9 class No. 714 (E. Pouteau).

Bournemouth express passing Wimbledon about 1905; L12 class 4-4-0 No. 434 (R.W. King).

were by no means confined to the lines west of Salisbury, and worked semi-fast trains on the Southampton line for more than thirty years. The next two classes, in 1903, were in effect also a pair: the S11 4-4-0 with 6 ft. driving wheels, intended for the West of England lines, and the L12, an express version with 6 ft. 7 in. wheels. Both classes appeared in many guises, with and without superheaters, with Urie boilers, with bogie tenders or six-wheeled; in SR days they were still to be seen on heavy trains on all three Sections, more in evidence than their numbers (10 S11s and 20 L12s) would suggest. They were often confused with the D15s of 1912, Drummond's last 4-4-0 class, ten of which were built to handle the heavier trains on the Bournemouth line. On this line, the yardstick for locomotive performance for most observers was the 16 miles up at 1 in 245 to 1 in 260 between mile-posts 72 and 56 in the Up direction. The D15 class 4-4-0s, studied by Cecil J. Allen in the December 1914 *Railway Magazine*, were deemed to have done well in averaging 47 mph between Winchester and Micheldever. These engines were handling the Bournemouth 2-hour expresses, and No. 466 is shown as arriving at Waterloo with half-a-minute in hand on the 9.8 non-stop. In Mr. Allen's view the booked time of 28 minutes for the 25¾ miles from Eastleigh to Basingstoke was impossible, and keeping time required very fast running on the downhill section; in this case the D15 managed to average 66 mph from Basingstoke to Clapham Junction.

Meanwhile, Drummond had made an attempt, not very successfully, to introduce more powerful engines, with five small classes of 4-cylinder 4-6-0 between 1905 and 1912; the last class, the T14 or 'Paddlebox' was used on some fast Bournemouth trains. Drummond was succeeded by R.W. Urie in 1912. His H15, N15 and S15 classes of 4-6-0 were all continued later by Maunsell, the N15 forming the first of the 'King Arthur' class of SR days. Before concluding the L&SWR survey, mention must be made of tank engines; there were many classes, first the 2-4-0T, several 4-4-2Ts, a 0-6-0T and 0-4-0T, and three classes of 0-4-4T, all seen on local work or shunting along the Southampton line. Urie's large tanks, the 4-6-2T and 4-8-0T were for other duties, but because any engine out-shopped from Eastleigh might make a proving run to Southampton, the 4-6-2Ts did appear at times. (This would no doubt be the reason for the surprise appearance in 1932 of a class W 2-6-4T on a passenger train at Southampton.)

When Maunsell took over as CME on the formation of the Southern Railway, the weight of holiday traffic to the West was increasing very rapidly, and without waiting to develop his own ideas, he immediately commissioned a large extension of the N15 4-6-0: ten were built at Eastleigh in 1925 (E448-457), taking the inside-bearing bogie tenders of the small 'Paddleboxes' which they replaced; thirty were built by North British also in 1925, and 13 more at Eastleigh in 1926/7 (E763-806). At the same time the twenty Urie N15s built in 1918–23 (E736-755) were made part of the 'King Arthur' class, though retaining their stove-pipe chimneys. Meanwhile, the prototype of the 'Lord Nelson' class had come out, a larger 4-cylinder design; fifteen more were built in 1928/9. However, only seven of these were allotted to the Western Section, and those on the Bournemouth line were mostly seen on the 'Belle' after its introduction. Several experimental changes were made in this class; however, the only very obvious one was the fitting of No. 857 in 1937 with a round-topped firebox.

The way in which the engines were worked—that is, hard—comes out in a description by a driver in the Southern Railway Magazine in 1939. The engine in question was No. 752, *Linette*, based at Eastleigh. Excerpts from this story are as follows:

"At 2 a.m. the Loco Running Foreman is asking whether the engine for Duty 280 has come in yet. The engine, No. 752, comes in having concluded its Thursday work by running light from Southampton... the shed engine-men turn the engine on the triangle (the turntable was only 54'10", unsuitable for the King Arthur class) and work her to her appointed pit road for attention by repair and cleaning staff. At 5.20 a.m. the train enginemen sign on... at 6.15 the Running Foreman watches the engine with cylinder cocks open slowly move from the shed for another day's outing of 20 hours.

"At 7.13 a.m. the Havre Boat Train steams away from the Channel Islands berth in a grand manner... the train becomes the only object of interest to the public as it crosses Canute Road, eight minutes late due to Customs. The boiler is at 180 lbs.... the load is light, only 262 tons. The driver works up the bank to Litchfield with 35% cut-off and regulator ¾ open and the schedule is maintained without difficulty. After leaving Basingstoke the engine is worked on a lighter cut-off... speed reaches 75–80 mph past Woking Junction... to Waterloo, reached at 9.5½, having made up 3½ minutes. The tender is again filled with water. No. 752 remains attached to the empty train and trails at rear to West London Sidings (to save a section) and then runs light to Nine Elms Loco Depot... it goes under the coal hopper... back to Waterloo for the 11.30 to Bournemouth."

He then describes how the engine takes a load of 379 tons to Winchester, where the crew is changed, and on to Bournemouth. After turning on the Branksome triangle, the tender is filled again and the engine runs light to Bournemouth West to work the 5.5 p.m. to Waterloo, then runs to Nine Elms for turning, and back to work the 10.30 p.m. to Southampton. "Total running some 400 miles, using 8 tons of coal and 15,000 gallons of water."

There have been many accounts over the years of footplate trips on the Southampton line; attention usually focuses on the only two real tests of performance: the six-mile pull up at 1 in 249 from near Basingstoke to the summit near Wootton signal box (near the 52¾-mile post), and the similar haul for Up trains already mentioned. The general impression given is that the earlier Drummond 4-6-0s could not be relied upon to keep time, but that the 'King Arthurs', whatever the driver's personal choice of cut-off, always had time in hand, and it was only the constant signal checks that prevented better performance. When first introduced, these engines had worried some drivers because of the way steam and smoke beat down on to the boiler front, obscuring the view. After various experiments with deflectors on the chimney, the problem was solved by fitting deflector plates beside the smoke-box, and from 1928 all the class (and others) were so fitted.

The remainder of Maunsell's regime was mainly occupied with rebuildings, and it could be said that the Southampton line had to make do with reach-me-downs. His 4-6-0 tender engine made from the ex-LBSC 'Remembrance' class 4-6-4Ts came on to the Bournemouth line in 1938, carrying names of locomotive engineers. After the Portsmouth line was electrified in 1937 a number of the 'Schools' class 4-4-0s were used on the Bournemouth run, though there had been doubts on water capacity for the non-stops. A few years earlier the U class 2-6-0s, some rebuilt from the 'River' class 2-6-4Ts, began to substitute for the Drummond 4-4-0s on semi-fast trains. There was at this time an enormous multiplicity of engine classes on the line, and no doubt the power classification letter painted on the front of the running plate (a system inherited from Urie) was useful. 'A' was the most powerful letter; when one came down to the 'F' on the 'Small Hoppers' (K10s) ability was clearly limited, and a certain amount of double-heading was practised, the pilot more often than not being an Adams outside-cylinder 4-4-0. However, good maintenance, the right coal, and skilful driving could do much; a 'Paddlebox' was noted on one occasion hauling 17 bogie carriages.

The southern section of the line saw a great many Great Western Railway engines, bringing trains via the former Didcot, Newbury & Southampton line; in the 'thirties the 'Dukes', 'Bulldogs' and 43xx 2-6-0s on these trains gave way mainly to 'Hall' 4-6-0s.

The outbreak of War in 1939 again brought special responsibilities, and with motive power being scarce nationwide, many inter-railway transferences took place. A curious switch in 1940 was of the two ex-LBSC J class 4-6-2Ts, which went on to the Waterloo–Basingstoke run. Being mostly fast to Woking, these two old gallopers from the pre-grouping Brighton expresses probably found this working more to their taste than their normal duty of stopping trains to Tunbridge Wells West. An interesting item in 1943 was the trial of Bulleid's new C1 class 0-6-0 on a 1,000-ton train between Woking and Basingstoke.

At the end of the War, the Southampton line was not badly off for locomotive power for the new peacetime services. While some of the engines in use on secondary trains were forty years old, most of those available for express work were 20 years old or less. The pattern was therefore very much as pre-War; in 1946 the new 'Merchant Navy' Pacific No. 21C2 had a trial on the Bournemouth trains, and after 1950 they were used at times, but were mainly on the Salisbury line. The newly-built 'West Country' and 'Battle of Britain' Pacifics were also confined mainly to other areas. Nationalisation in 1948 brought little change; by 1950 there were still T9 4-4-0s and 'Paddlebox' 4-6-0s on the Bournemouth run. However, next year came a foretaste of change, when BR 'Britannia' class 4-6-2 70009 *Alfred the Great* did some duties, and in 1953 even the Midland Region Co-Co diesels Nos. 10001/2 were tried out, together with Standard Class 4 2-6-0s on semi-fast work. This was in a year when the 'Merchant Navy' class was temporarily withdrawn for crank-shaft checks, and some unusual engines had to be

COMPARATIVE DETAILS OF SELECTED LOCOMOTIVE CLASSES USED ON THE SOUTHAMPTON LINE

Date	Class		Cylinders	Driving wheels ft. ins.		Weight (tons) in working order
1839		2-2-2	13×18	5	6	
1855	'Saxon'	2-4-0	15½×24	5	0	54½
1862	'Eagle'	2-2-2	17×22	6	0	53¼
1864	'Fireball'	2-2-2	17×22	7	0	59¼
1874	302	0-6-0	17×24	5	1	54¾
1879	380	4-4-0	18×24	5	7	76½
1881	395	0-6-0	17½×26	5	1	66
1883	445	4-4-0	18×26	7	1	78½
1887	A12	0-4-2	19×26	6	0	87
1890	X2	4-4-0	19×26	7	1	81¾
1895	T6	4-4-0	19×26	7	1	83¼
1899	T9	4-4-0	18½×26	6	7	93¾ ††
1903	L11	4-4-0	18½×26	5	7	95½ ††
1904	L12	4-4-0	18½×26	6	7	99††
1912	T14	4-6-0	15×26★	6	7	131
1912	D15	4-4-0	19½×26	6	7	108¾ ††
1913	H15	4-6-0	21×28	6	0	128½
1918	N15	4-6-0	22×28	6	7	134¾
1926	E124	4-6-0	16×26★	6	7	140¼
1930	V	4-4-0	16½×26†	6	7	109½
1935	N15X	4-6-0	21×28	6	9	130
1941	MN	4-6-2	18×24†	6	2	135¼
1945	WC	4-6-2	16¾×26†	6	2	128¾

★4 cylinders
†3 cylinders   ††when with bogie tender

The above figures are not comprehensive: most types were rebuilt at various times to differing weights, and several were fitted with more than one type of tender.

---

brought in, including an Eastern Region V2 2-6-2 which worked semi-fasts to Southampton. 1955 saw further experiments; 'Schools' class 4-4-0 30932 with a built-up tender was run from Waterloo to Bournemouth non-stop. The next year saw some of the rebuilt 'Merchant Navy' class at work, and it seemed somewhat sad when in 1959 several Standard Class 5 4-6-0s went to work bearing the names (though new name-plates) off the earlier series of 'King Arthur' class engines, which were being scrapped after 35 years of hard work. This class, and the 'Nelsons' and to some extent the 'Schools' had been the mainstay of the Southampton line, with the various mixed traffic 4-6-0s used on relief work; as they were phased out the romantic era of Southern steam ended. Hereafter a hotch-potch of engines would work the line, often one shedded far away and working a turn for convenience, or after repair at Eastleigh — in 1965, for example, an 8F 2-8-0 and a Crewe-based 'Britannia' were seen. Probably the last 'Arthur' to work regularly was *Sir Priamus* which was still rostered in 1962. An interesting brief return to glory was in the same year, when the T9 4-4-0 No. 120 restored to L&SWR livery worked between London and Basingstoke.

In 1965, a Western Region Type 4 diesel worked a boat train to Southampton, via Guildford and Cosham; meanwhile, the Exeter line was receiving 'Warship' class diesels. Next year some Brush Type 4s were seen, and Type 3s became common. From Bournemouth to Weymouth, Hymek diesels took over. Steam on the Exeter trains finished (regular rostering) on 29 November 1965. Such steam as was still on the Southampton line was in sorry state; cleaning and maintenance were poor, and failures frequent: the Bulleid Pacifics seemed to be most accident-prone. The last regular steam on the Waterloo to Weymouth line was on 9 July 1967, when 'Merchant Navy' No. 35030 pulled into Waterloo, facing enthusiasts with the prospect that very soon nothing would be seen on the Southampton line other than what many thought of as tramcars — the EMUs.

ELECTRIC ROLLING STOCK

When planning 'new' stock for the Bournemouth electrification, the authorities followed previous Southern Railway practice in incorporating a great deal of existing steam-hauled stock rather than building all-new. However, as described earlier, the basic plan was revolutionary for this country, relying on long trains at high speed being propelled in one direction, while the inter-availability of all the various types of unit involved was also basic; that is ordinary EMUs (4-VEP), high-powered 'tractor' units (4-REP), and diesel-electric and electro-diesel locomotives.

The first trains to go into service were twenty 4-VEP sets (7701-20) for semi-fast service. As a temporary measure one peculiar set was made up (No. 8001). This was really two sets, one of five coaches (driving trailer-motor-buffet-motor-driving trailer) and one of three (driving trailer-motor-driving trailer). By 1974 this had been re-vamped as two VEPs. For the fast services, eleven 4-REPs were provided; these contained two motor seconds each having two motor bogies, four traction motors of 365 hp in each coach, rated to be able to propel two four-coach trailer units (4-TCs). Initially, some of the trailer sets were built as 2nd-only 3-TC, but strengthened later. (Nos. 301-3, becoming 429-31). In 1974, four more REPs, Nos. 3012-5, were added to the original 3001-11, and 4-TCs 432-4 added to the original 401-31.

In the early days all kinds of combinations were to be seen, but the standard train comprised a REP at the London end propelling (in the Down direction) two TCs, one of which would on arrival at Bournemouth be hauled on to Weymouth by a class 33, being propelled back to attach to the rear of the London train at Bournemouth.

To work the Ocean Liner trains, which had to pass beyond the limit of the live rail, ten Southern Region electric locomotives were converted at Crewe to 2,500 hp electro-diesels in 1966 (class 74), Nos. E6101-10. These duties were, however, shared with class 33 diesel-electrics and class 73 electro-diesels.

DOCKS LOCOMOTIVES

The locomotives serving the docks railways were taken over by the L&SWR with the Port, but were kept on a separate register and retained their names; replacement engines were also named for a time. The following were acquired (the condensing engines had been purchased before the take-over of the Docks); numbers later allotted are shown:

	Canute (Dick & Stephenson)	118 *Vulcan* (Vulcan Foundry)
	Sir Bevis (Shanks)	408 *Bretwalda* (Vulcan Foundry)
	Ascupert (Shanks)	457 *Clausentum* (Hawthorn)
	Arbroath (Shanks)	458 *Ironside* (Hawthorn)
108	*Cowes* (Shanks; condensing)	
109	*Southampton* (Shanks; condensing)	
110	*Ritzebuttel* (Shanks; condensing)	

All were 0-4-0ST types. To replace some and increase capacity, the L&SWR provided 12 B4 class 0-4-0T engines as follows:

81 *Jersey*	93 *St. Malo*	102 *Granville*
85 *Alderney*	95 *Honfleur*	176 *Guernsey*
86 *Havre*	96 *Normandy*	101 *Dinan* (added 1922)
89 *Trouville*	97 *Brittany*	147 *Dinard* (added 1922)
90 *Caen*	98 *Cherbourg*	

Somewhat later, two C14 class 0-4-0T engines, a post-war conversion of the unsuccessful 2-2-0T railmotor engines, were added, Nos. 0741 and 0744; however, these were not named and did not come under Docks control. In the early 'thirties the Drummond inspection railcar 58S was stationed in the Docks to carry notables around the new works; it was coupled to an ex-SECR 6w. saloon.

Some of the old docks shunters enjoyed a further life as shed pilots after leaving the docks; *Clausentum*, now numbered E734, was at Guildford for many years.

After the last War, the B4s began to be displaced by 'USA' 0-6-0Ts (Nos. 30061-74), assisted from 1961 by some E1 and E2 0-6-0Ts of the former LBSC. In 1962, the first of a series of 275 hp diesel shunters arrived (D2995/6), fitted with two-way radio in the cabs. There was some overlap — B4 No. 30102 was still there in 1963, and until the general end of steam some of the 'USA's were in use.

It would seem that the dock locomotives were subject to marine law; there is a story, probably true, that one B4 was seen in a siding with its motion officially sealed after the driver had been found carrying contraband.

CARRIAGE STOCK

The first carriages comprised three-compartment first-class carrying 18 (three a side); 3-compartment seconds carrying 24 (four a side), and also some seconds seating 30, probably four-compartment ones with some space allotted to a brake. The 'excursion carriages' were no doubt fitted with wooden benches, but may have been roofed. Each carriage weighed around 4 tons, making the normal six-coach train about the same weight as one modern coach. By 1860 there was better provision for the increasing number of third class passengers, and some 5-compartment thirds were provided in a style popular (with managements!) at the time, with outside body framing and tongued-and-grooved boarding inside, half-height compartment divisions and two lamps to be shared by all compartments. The first four-wheelers in typical L&SWR body style arrived in the 'seventies, and shortly afterwards the first six-wheelers, put on to the fast trains to steady the motion. These included some tri-composites, an arrangement the L&SWR was rather proud of. The four-wheelers were 22–26 feet in length, and the six-wheelers 30–34 feet. Arc-roofed bogie carriages (on 'American' type bogies) were on the trains by 1883, some of which were still working in the Isle of Wight sixty years later. The elliptical-roofed bogies of 1889–92 finally got rid of the restricted interior height, and set a style which remained with new building for over twenty years, so that the L&SWR trains were notable over the years for the neatness of appearance, roof-lines being the same throughout the train, which was certainly not true of a number of railways. The luxury of lavatories for 1st and 2nd class passengers was the next step, and in 1898 some 48-foot tri-compos had lavatory access from all classes; the arrangement was 3/Lav/3/1/Lav/1/2/Lav/2; 3rd compartments were 6 feet wide, 2nds 6 ft. $1\frac{1}{2}$ ins and 1sts 6 ft. 10 ins. Gas-lighting instead of oil was used from 1908.

As stated earlier, Pullman cars were in limited use from 1880. In 1903, Eastleigh produced its first dining-car trains, each made up of four converted Eagle carriages and a new 'cooking car' — however, it is doubtful if these were used on the Bournemouth line. Dining cars proper were built from 1906 onwards, with clerestore roofs; the catering for these was in the hands of Messrs. Spiers & Pond, who held the contract until 1931 when Frederick Hotels took over. The 56 foot dining cars weighed 32 tons and seated 11 in a 1st saloon and 17 in the 2nd/3rd saloon, the kitchen being between. New full-corridor coaches of 54–56 feet were built to go with them, and some were allotted to the 12.30 and 7.20 Down Bournemouth trains. In 1906, W. Panter had succeeded Surrey Warner as carriage superintendent, but he did not at first alter the body styling. He produced a number of brake coaches with long luggage compartments, the 1908 construction having only 3 passenger compartments; this ample provision allowed the vans which had previously been attached at each end of expresses to be discontinued.

In 1918, second class was abolished. New construction begun before 1914, was somewhat limited but it was in a completely new style, with rounded sides and steel panels. Four 5-coach pantry sets of this type were built in 1921 for the Bournemouth service; they ran on wide plate-type bogies and because of their heavy appearance were known as 'Ironclads'. Some special stock for the Southampton boat trains included two Pantry Brake Firsts with the arrangement Lav/1/1/1/Pantry/Bk.

In common with most other lines, the L&SWR had long formed its suburban stock into close-coupled sets; the so-called Bogie Blocks of four coaches joined by a central bar carried much of the main line semi-fast traffic until the 'twenties, when they started to be broken into 2-coach push-pull sets. The L&SWR extended the system to its long-distance stock also, and the pre-war straight-sided corridor stock was mostly formed into 3-coach sets. The system was continued in SR days; the L&SWR sets kept their old numbers (painted in large numerals on the ends of the set), the SECR and LBSC sets being renumbered from 501 on.

When Maunsell took over as CME of the Southern Railway, he continued the Panter construction of corridor coaches for a while, though he substituted the SECR type bogie for the 'Ironclad'. By 1926, coaches were coming out in a recognisably different Maunsell style, still mostly in 3-coach sets. They had end connectors which were similar to those on Pullman cars, so Pullmans could be cut in at any point. From then on the corridor sets were continually cut about and made into sets of 2, 3, 4, 5 and 8 coaches, so that any general statement about them would be impossible. A large number of 'loose' coaches were also built, including the 'non-descripts', open saloons which could be 1st or 3rd, or used as dining or tea cars. The most notable production perhaps was in 1938, two eleven-coach trains for the Bournemouth service, made up from shorter sets, and painted a new light green — some 'Schools' class engines were similarly painted to go with them. For some reason the SR presented these to the public as entirely new trains; they were indeed comprehensively re-styled inside. They weighed 352 tons and carried 102 1st and 408 3rd class passengers.

O.V.S. Bulleid took over as CME in 1937, but was able to do little until 1945, when some new carriages with his styling — welded steel bodies with round-cornered windows — appeared with the old body length of 59 feet, shortly to be increased to a standard $64\frac{1}{2}$ feet. Again, they were in 3-coach sets, and some went on to the 7.21 a.m. Up and 3.20 pm Down Bournemouth service. His next production included coaches with centre vestibule and end doors, and in 1947, eleven 6-coach sets were built for the Bournemouth service, comprising 3rd Bk (semi-open) — corridor compo — 1st diner — kitchen and 3rd diner — 3rd (open) — 3rd Bk (semi-open). Under the BR regime, some of these trains were painted in the 'plum-and-spilt-milk' livery followed later by the red-and-cream; but some were painted or re-painted in green, so that for some years any train might present a rather varied appearance. The last Bulleid carriage was built in 1951 and thereafter standard BR stock was adopted when required; however, the Bulleid and to some extent, the Maunsell stock continued in use for many years, though from 1966 the concept of set trains was abandoned. Even after the electrification in 1967, some Bulleid stock continued on the Boat Trains. There must have been considerable difficulties in rostering at this time, as the available stock included carriages with steam, electric or dual heating, and vacuum or air brakes.

Mention should be made of other passenger train stock. The L&SWR parcels and guard's vans followed the same progress as the other stock, from four to six and finally bogie. Early examples had lantern roof look-outs, which gave way to end duckets (often one at each end) or centre duckets. Some bogie vans had the words 'Bullion Van' painted clearly on the sole-bar, a strange invitation to the thief. Others were lettered 'Fruit'. There was a very heavy seasonal fruit traffic from Hampshire, and to cope with it a number of old four-wheeled passenger sets were converted with seats stripped out and 'Fruit' painted on the frames. Milk traffic was also extensive, and milk trains in later days might include either 4 or 6w. milk vans with slatted sides, milk tank wagons, or flat-wagons carrying road milk tanks. In general, the L&SWR preferred to run complete van trains, including gas-container wagons, some empty stock, service vans, etc. rather than adding them to slow trains as some other lines did.

Apart from the early years of the century, Pullmans were not used again on Bournemouth trains until the 'Bournemouth Belle' started running in 1931. The first 'Belle' was made up from four new cars, Nos. 81-84, an older 8-wheel No. 60, two twelve-wheelers Nos. 40 and 41, and three first class cars, *Flora*, *Montana*, and *Aurelia*. There were some changes over the years; the final stock comprised five second class cars, four firsts, and a bogie van at each end. From 1 January 1931, Pullmans were also used on the Ocean Liner trains, usually three at a time and cut into the middle, but on relief trains they sometimes appeared singly as first or last carriage.

Following electrification, some locomotive-hauled stock has had to be kept on the line for the Channel Islands and Ocean Liner trains, the cross-country services and excursion trains. The 4-TC sets are sometimes used not in electric formations, and have also been seen off the line, working to Salisbury and even to Bristol and Kensington (Olympia).

THE SHIPS

It is necessary to give a brief survey of the vessels employed on the railway-owned services from Southampton to France and the Channel Islands, since they were the reason for much of the attention focused on the line. There had been a mail service to the Channel Islands from the port from 1794, and when the railway arrived there was a certain amount of passenger traffic being dealt with by private operators. At that time, railways were not allowed to operate ships; however, in 1848, Parliament gave permission for the L&SWR to own ships, a facility not taken up until 1862. To bridge the gap, a company called 'South Western Steam Navigation Co.' was formed, in 1845, using two almost new wooden vessels off the Weymouth service, 'South Western' and 'Transit' and an iron boat 'Wonder.' Following this, new and larger boats came on with great rapidity. It may seem strange that so many were acquired for such relatively small traffic. There are two reasons: one, several boats foundered at various times on the notorious Casquets rocks. Second, development in terms of speed and comfort was rapid, and the railway could not afford to lag behind. The early boats were mostly paddle-steamers; 'Wolf' of 1897 was the last 'paddler', though as early as 1850 the 'Caesarea' and 'Sarnia' were screw-driven (they also had a full rig of sails as well). These two displaced only 265 tons and carried 60 berth passengers; they would have been pressed to maintain 14 knots. For people tossing about in what were often very rough seas, eager only to get their feet on land, a few knots extra were gold-dust. By 1881, the 'Dora' was doing 16 knots, and by 1894, the 'Columbia' 19 knots. The 1910 'Caesarea' was a turbine vessel capable of over 20 knots, and by 1931, the 'Isle of Sark' of 2,211 tons could have done 25 knots — though the long sea crossings, unlike the Straits services, by now placed less emphasis on speed and more on comfort. This vessel carried 1,500 passengers.

Some of the French ports had the disadvantage of not being able to be entered at all states of the tide; it was not until 1931 that the service to St. Malo became non-tidal. In the same year the service which had terminated at the rather rustic landing-place at Ouistreham was extended into Caen. A further feature of the early 'thirties was the use of some of the steamers as cruise ships; the 'St. Briac' ran regular cruises to Rouen. The following list gives the vessels built for the passenger services up to the last War. After the War, things changed very much, with the growth of roll-on services for cars, and the later vast increase of services across the Straits, including Hovercraft. Then in the 'sixties services to France ceased and the Channel Islands services were moved to Weymouth, and this particular part of Southampton's railway history came to an end.

Mention should be made of the very valuable War work of the vessels; in the last War, the 'Isle of Sark' was the last ship to leave Guernsey before the Germans came in 1940, and the 'Hantonia' the last civilian ship to leave St. Malo. Thereafter War work took the Southampton ships to strange places, including India, Africa, and the Panama Canal.

1845	South Western★	1870	Alice★	1905	Ada
	Transit★		Fanny★		Bertha
	Wonder	1871	Wolf	1906	Princess Ena
1848	Grand Turk	1874	South Western	1910	Caesarea
	Courier		Hilda		Sarnia
	Dispatch	1881	Dora	1911	Hantonia
	Express		Ella		Normannia
1850	Caesarea	1885	Laura	1920	Ardena
	Sarnia	1890	Frederica		Larina★
1855	Alliance		Lydia	1924	Dinard
1856	Havre		Stella		St. Briac
1860	Southampton	1894	Columbia	1930	Isle of Jersey
1863	Normandy		Alma		Isle of Guernsey
1864	Brittany	1898	Vera	1931	Isle of Sark
1865	Dumfries	1900	Alberta	1933	Brittany
1867	Granville★				

Vessels asterisked (★) were second-hand.

HEADCODES

In common with most railways in the south of England, the L&SWR used a system of daytime headcodes to describe trains, paralleling the use of lamps at night. It was less complex than some, comprising the use of white diamond-shaped and white round discs, white discs with red or black crosses, and a 'special' disc which was white with a large black centre blob. Initially, Southampton and Bournemouth line trains showed at the funnel a red cross, later a white diamond. From 1911 on, the codes comprised white discs at the funnel and both smokebox-side irons, and Terminus trains a white disc on the nearside smokebox iron. The 'special' disc was carried also by Ocean Liner trains, at the nearside buffer iron. When the SR took over, the Bournemouth line code was altered to white discs at the offside buffer and nearside smokebox.

On electrification, the route numbers allotted were: 90, Weymouth Boat Trains, 91 Bournemouth fast, 92 semi-fast, 93 stopping.

SOURCES

To supplement my own notes from visits to the line and the Docks over fifty years, I have had recourse to various notes in *The Railway Magazine, The Southern Railway Magazine* (notably the writings of the late F.E. Box); also Dendy Marshall's official history of the Southern Railway, the late R.H. Clark's 'Southern Region Record', various notices issued by the Docks Authority, 'Bradshaw', Southern Railway and L&SWR Timetables, and F. Burtt's 'L&SWR Locomotives' of 1948.

STATION OPENING AND CLOSING DATES

OPENED

	Waterloo	11 July 1848	
1¼m	Vauxhall	11 July 1848	
	Nine Elms	21 May 1838	Closed 11 July 1848.
2¾m	Queens Road	1 Nov. 1877	
4m	Clapham Junction	2 March 1863	
4½m	Clapham Common	21 May 1838	Wandsworth until Aug. 1846. Closed 2 March 1863.
5½m	Earlsfield	1 April 1884	
7¼m	Wimbledon	21 May 1848	
8¾m	Raynes Park	30 Oct. 1871	
9¾m	Malden	Dec. 1846	
11m	Berrylands	16 Oct. 1933	
12m	Surbiton	21 May 1838	As Kingston; Surbiton & Kingston from 1 July 1863; Surbiton from May 1977.
14½m	Esher	21 May 1838	As Ditton Marsh.
16m	Hersham	28 Sept. 1936	
17m	Walton	21 May 1838	
19m	Weybridge	21 May 1838	
20½m	Byfleet	10 July 1927	As West Weybridge until 12 June 1961.
21¾m	West Byfleet	Dec. 1887	Byfleet until May 1914.
24¼m	Woking	21 May 1838	As Woking Common to 1843.
28m	Brookwood	1864	
33¼m	Farnborough	24 Sept. 1838	
35m	Bramshot Halt	10 May 1913	Golf platform; public from 1938; closed 1946.
36½m	Fleet	1847	Fleetpond until 1 July 1869.
40m	Winchfield	24 Sept. 1838	As Shapley Heath.
42½m	Hook	2 July 1883	
47¾m	Basingstoke	10 June 1839	
58m	Micheldever	11 May 1840	As Andover Road until Feb. 1856.
66½m	Winchester	10 June 1839	Winchester City until 10 July 1969.
69¾m	Shawford	1 Sept. 1882	
73½m	Eastleigh	10 June 1839	Bishopstoke until July 1889.
75m	Southampton Airport	1 April 1966	On site of Atlantic Park Hostel Halt, 30 October 1929 to ?
75¾m	Swaythling	15 Oct. 1883	
77¼m	St. Denys	1 May 1861	Portwood until 1 Jan. 1876.
78½m	Northam	1 Dec. 1872	Closed 5 Sept. 1966.
79m	Southampton Terminus	10 June 1839	Southampton to July 1858, Southampton Docks to Sept. 1896, Town and Docks to Nov. 1912, Town for Docks to 9 July 1923; closed 5 Sept. 1966.
79¼m	Southampton Central	1 June 1847	Blechynden to July 1858, West to 7 July 1935; resited 1895.
	Royal Pier	Jan. 1891	Closed Sept. 1914.
	Ocean Terminal	31 July 1950	Last used 1 Dec. 1980.

P2